NATIONAL
GEOGRAPHIC

# Volcano!

## PATHFINDER EDITION

By Beth Geiger

## CONTENTS

# Volcano!

Volcanoes are some of the hottest places on Earth. They are also some of the coolest.

*Kilauea, Hawaii*

# By Beth Geiger

J oanne Green carefully put her foot down as if it were her last step. It could have been. The hardened **lava** underfoot was blazing hot. A nearby river of glowing lava splashed melted rock.

"The heat on your face is very, very intense," said Green. "If you aren't careful," she went on, "you'll melt your boots on the hot rock. Or worse!"

Green, you see, is a **volcanologist.** She's a scientist who studies volcanoes. To learn about these superheated spots, she gets as close to them as she can.

## Towering Infernos

Green was studying Kilauea. It's a volcano in Hawaii. It's just one of nearly 600 volcanoes on Earth's land. Many more rise from the ocean floor. All together, there are 1,500 active volcanoes worldwide.

Active volcanoes, however, make up only a small fraction of all mountains of fire. Many others are dormant, or "sleeping." These volcanoes haven't erupted in a long time. Some may never erupt again. Then there are extinct volcanoes. They fizzled out thousands or even millions of years ago.

All kinds of volcanoes—active, dormant, or extinct—are important. Volcanoes made 80 percent of Earth's surface. Most of our fertile soils came from volcanoes. And much of the air we breathe was erupted by them.

## It's About the Lava

A volcano is an opening, or **vent,** into Earth's hot interior. Molten rock, or **magma,** rises through the vent. When the magma blasts onto Earth's surface, it's called lava.

Not all lava is the same. Some volcanoes make runny lava. It flows very fast, like pancake batter. Runny lava forms a gentle slope called a shield volcano.

Other volcanoes erupt thick, sticky lava. It flows slowly, like toothpaste. This kind of lava cannot flow very far. It forms a mountain with steep slopes. It's called a composite volcano.

Composite volcanoes can erupt violently. A blast can hurl ash and lava at more than 600 miles per hour. Sometimes an eruption blows away large chunks of the volcano itself. All that's left is a steaming **caldera.**

**Real Fireworks.** *Lava explodes as it hits the Pacific Ocean. The molten rock flowed downhill from Kilauea, a volcano in Hawaii.*

**Busy Place.** TOP: *Kilauea has been erupting since 1983. It's the most active volcano on Earth.* ABOVE: *Cooling lava forms rock. That's how the Hawaiian Islands developed.*

# The Ring of Fire

Three-quarters of all volcanoes rise near the rim of the Pacific Ocean. This circle of hot spots is called the Ring of Fire (see map).

It's no accident that so many volcanoes are located there. The Ring of Fire is an area where some of the plates that form Earth's surface meet.

Sometimes when plates meet, one of them moves under the other. The lower one melts, forming magma. This magma squeezes through cracks in the surrounding rock. The magma can then burst through Earth's surface to build a new volcano or erupt from an old one.

NG MAPS

## Living With a Volcano

All active volcanoes affect the plants and animals that live around them. They make rich soils for plants to grow in. The plants attract all kinds of animals. Volcanoes even change the way people live. Farmers grow crops on rich volcanic soils. Tourists vacation near the beautiful mountains. Cities grow in the valleys beneath the peaks.

But life near an active volcano isn't easy. Sometimes the peaks turn into dangerous mountains of fire. When that happens, you don't want to be anywhere nearby.

## A Sleeping Giant Awakens

One of the most scenic U.S. volcanoes was Mount St. Helens. It's about 95 miles south of Seattle, Washington. The mighty mountain had last erupted in 1857.

Over the years, millions of people moved to the area around Mount St. Helens. Thousands more visited each year.

After all, the snowcapped volcano seemed peaceful and calm. But that all changed on the morning of May 18, 1980. At 8:32 a.m. a powerful earthquake rattled the area. Suddenly the north side of the volcano exploded.

**Blowing Its Top.** *An old photo shows visitors how Mount St. Helens looked before May 1980.*

## Changing Land

Hot ash and steam surged down the volcanic slopes at 200 miles per hour. When the smoke cleared, it looked like the top of the mountain had been chopped off. More than 1,000 feet was gone. A swath of land stretching 15 miles from the volcano was destroyed.

Today the volcano continues to erupt. But now it is slowly rebuilding itself. One day in the distant future, it will look much like it used to. But it is destined to repeat its violent past and destroy itself again.

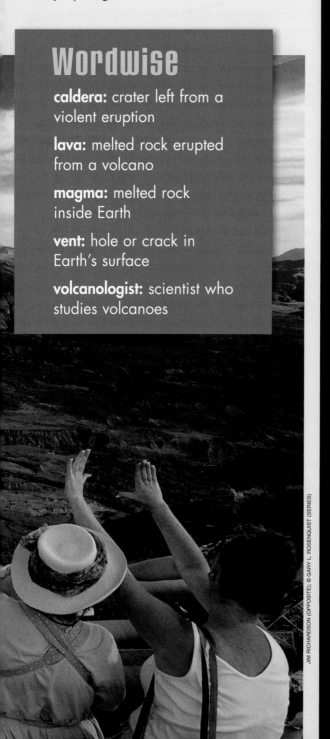

## Wordwise

**caldera:** crater left from a violent eruption

**lava:** melted rock erupted from a volcano

**magma:** melted rock inside Earth

**vent:** hole or crack in Earth's surface

**volcanologist:** scientist who studies volcanoes

# Mount St. Helens Erupts

MAY 18, 1980 • 8:27:00 A.M.
**Picture–Perfect?** *Mount St. Helens looked calm and peaceful. It wasn't. Scientists knew something would happen. But no one knew exactly when.*

MAY 18, 1980 • 8:32:37 A.M.
**The Bad Beginning.** *The mountain exploded at 8:32 a.m. Ash soared 60,000 feet into the air.*

MAY 18, 1980 • 8:32:51 A.M.
**Dark Day.** *The blast produced 400 million tons of dust. It blanketed 230 square miles.*

# Inside a Volcano

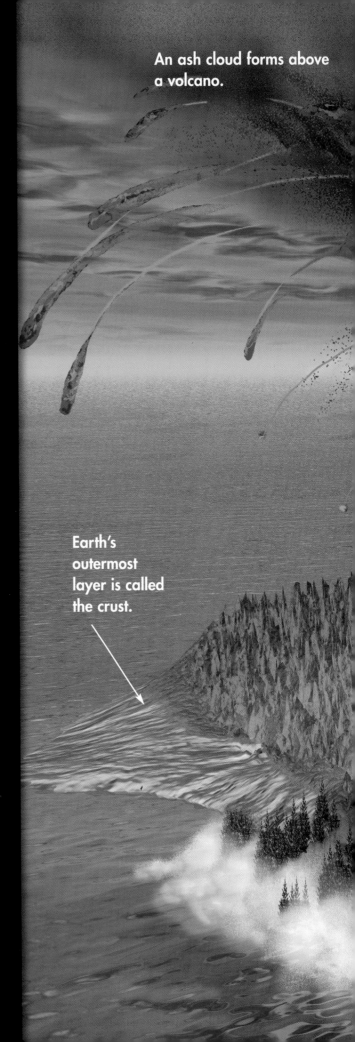

An ash cloud forms above a volcano.

Earth's outermost layer is called the crust.

**M**ost people think that volcanoes are simply large mountains that erupt lava. But a volcano actually starts deep beneath Earth's surface, or crust.

The layer below the crust is called the mantle. It is very hot. The heat can melt rock. Sometimes pressure forces this heated rock through cracks in the crust. This can form a volcano.

Volcanoes form on all Earth's continents, even icy Antarctica. The mountains of fire also rise from the ocean floor.

Use the diagram to learn about the different parts of a volcano.

Lava is molten rock that flows from a volcano.

A crater is the opening at the top of a volcano.

Molten rock rises through the central vent.

Magma is molten rock inside a volcano.

A magma chamber lies deep inside a volcano.

ARTWORK BY PRECISION GRAPHICS

# Hawaii
## Island Chain

**F**or many people, Hawaii is a lush, green paradise. But this chain of islands has a red-hot history. The islands are made of lava. They formed from underwater volcanoes in the Pacific Ocean.

## Hot Spot

The Hawaiian Islands sit near a superheated area of Earth's crust. Temperatures under the crust are so high there that they can actually melt rock. Scientists call this area the Hawaiian hot spot.

For millions of years, the Hawaiian hot spot has melted holes through the Pacific Plate. This plate is one of the largest in Earth's crust. It makes up the floor of the vast Pacific Ocean.

Like other plates, the Pacific Plate moves slowly. It travels about 10 centimeters a year. It slides directly over the Hawaiian hot spot.

## Volcanoes, Old and New

Five million years ago, the hot spot burned a hole through the Pacific Plate. Magma, or hot rock, spilled out onto the ocean floor. Over time, this rock piled up into a giant mound. At last, it jutted out of the ocean. The island of Kauai was born!

Kauai was the first Hawaiian Island to form. It wasn't the last. Over many years, the Pacific Plate carried Kauai past the hot spot.

But the hot spot kept burning. As the plate moved, it scorched new holes in the crust. New mounds grew from the ocean floor. Each mound formed another island.

Today, most of the islands have moved past the hot spot. Their volcanoes are now extinct. Only the island of Hawaii is still erupting. Someday, it too will grow quiet. Yet the hot spot will continue to burn— and to form new islands.

**Hot History.** *Kauai is the oldest of the Hawaiian Islands. This chain of islands formed over a hot spot on the ocean floor.*

## How the Islands Formed

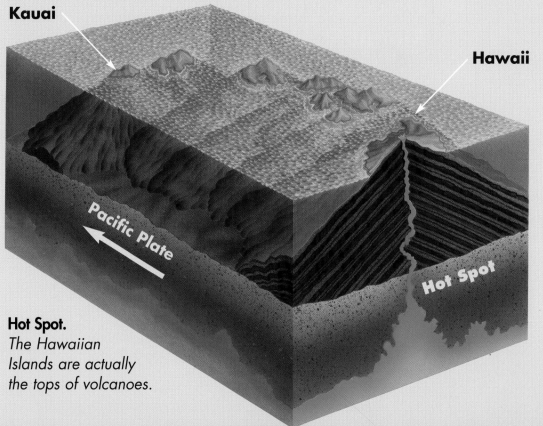

**Kauai**

**Hawaii**

Pacific Plate

Hot Spot

**Hot Spot.**
*The Hawaiian Islands are actually the tops of volcanoes.*

STEPHEN WAGNER (ILLUSTRATION); DAVID ALAN HARVEY (PHOTO).

# Volcanoes

Answer these questions to find out what you've learned about this hot topic.

**1** What is a volcanologist?

**2** How is magma different from lava?

**3** Why do so many volcanoes form along the Ring of Fire?

**4** Describe what happened when Mount St. Helens erupted.

**5** What are the differences between extinct, dormant, and active volcanoes?